D1422876

THE LITTLE BOOK OF
CRICKET

Published by OH!
20 Mortimer Street
London W1T 3JW

ISBN 978-1-91161-042-7

Editorial: Chris Caulfield, Victoria Godden
Project Manager: Russell Porter
Design: Andy Jones
Production: Rachel Burgess

A CIP catalogue for this book is available from the British Library

Printed in Dubai

10 9 8 7 6 5 4 3 2 1

Jacket cover photograph: Christos Georghiou/Shutterstock

THE LITTLE BOOK OF CRICKET

GENERAL EDITOR
CHRIS CAULFIELD

CONTENTS

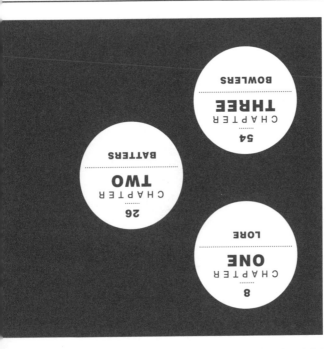

INTRODUCTION

Cricket: the feeling of summer and the sounds of leather on willow. An ancient pastime that brings generations together like few others can with tales of heroic centuries, whirlwind five-wicket hauls, game-changing overs and unplayable deliveries passed down from parent to child.

First codified in 1744 by "Noblemen and Gentlemen" at London's Artillery Ground, the game has been presided over by the Marylebone Cricket Club since its inception in 1787. The ghosts of cricket's past have always loomed large over the sport as new heroes rise up to add their names to the pantheon of greats, while others break new ground in formats the forefathers could never have imagined.

With every delivery fired down only adding to the lore, the legacy laid down by the guardians of cricket's great past have ensured the spirit of the game remains as true today as when the first ball was rolled towards two stumps.

That's not to say that cricket has stood still.

There have been six revisions of its famous rule book, which was originally written on a handkerchief, since 2000. The most recent reflects the skyrocketing popularity of the game among women and girls.

From the Test arena to its latest incarnation, The Hundred, via one-day internationals, four-day county championships and T20, there is enough cricket for the once-summer spectacle to be played all year round.

Cricket's excitement comes through leadership, friendship and teamwork, all of which create lasting bonds between different nationalities, cultures and religions. This is never more true than when the game is played within the mythic Spirit of Cricket.

This book, through the words of the greatest batsmen, bowlers and journalists ever involved in the game born in the villages of England, hopes to capture that spirit.

Chapter

1

• • • • • • •

LORE

" Who would think that a little bit of leather, and two pieces of wood, had such a delightful and delighting power! **"**

MARY RUSSELL MITFORD

Prose and Verse, 1841

"Now that the sun has rent his veil of gray.
And on the greensward plays with flashing chords.
From books and shaded hours let us away,
Let us to Lord's!**"**

GEORGE FRANCIS WILSON

"An invitation to Lord's", from Cricket Poems, *1905*

❝ [Cricket comprises] casting a ball at three straight sticks and defending the same with a fourth. **❞**

RUDYARD KIPLING

Collected Works of Rudyard Kipling, *2015*

"Cricket is certainly among the most powerful links which keep our Empire together. It is one of the greatest contributions which the British people have made to the cause of humanity.**"**

SIR RANJITSINHJI VIBHAJI JADEJA

Noted Indian Test cricketer who played for the England team and later became ruler of the Indian princely state of Nawanagar, The Imperial Game, *1998*

❝Cricket, however, has more in it than mere efficiency. There is something called the spirit of cricket, which cannot be defined.**❞**

LIONEL, LORD TENNYSON
Sticky Wickets, *1950*

"If Stalin had learned to play cricket the world might now be a better place to live in.**"**

DR R. DOWNEY

Archbishop of Liverpool, 1948

" 'I'm beginning to understand the game
scientifically. What a noble game it is, too!'
'Isn't it? But it's more than a game.
It's an institution,' said Tom.
'Yes,' said Arthur, 'the birthright of British
boys old and young, as habeas corpus and
trial by jury are of British men.' **"**

THOMAS HUGHES

Tom Brown's Schooldays, *1857*

16

❝ If I knew I was going to die today,
I'd still want to hear the cricket scores. **❞**

Attributed to **J. H. HARDY**

in C. P. Snow's foreword to A Mathematician's Apology, *1967*

"Few things are more deeply rooted in the collective imagination of the English than the village cricket match. It stirs a romantic illusion about the rustic way of life, it suggests a tranquil and unchanging order in an age of bewildering flux, and it persuades a lot of townsfolk that that is where they would rather be.**"**

GEOFFREY MOORHOUSE

The Best Loved Game, 1979

❝It may not be cricket, but it's four.❞

E. M. GRACE,

older brother of his famous sibling W.G., after pulling a ball from

outside off-stump, considered unethical in the mid-nineteenth

century (date unknown)

❝If there is a threat to the game of cricket,
that threat lies in the first-class arena.
One-day cricket, especially day-night cricket,
is here to stay. **❞**

SIR DONALD BRADMAN
Wisden, *1986*

" [One-day cricket] is injecting a dementia into the souls of those who play it. **"**

BILL O'REILLY

Sydney Morning Herald, *1981*

"The dot ball has become the Holy Grail. "

COLIN COWDREY

1982 (source unknown)

"A sell-out with rosettes, singing, cheers, jeers and countercheers … this may not have been cricket to the purists, but by golly it was just the stuff the doctor ordered.**"**

PETER WILSON *of the* Daily Mirror
on the first Gillette Cup final, which Sussex won by fourteen runs in 1963

❝This 'instant cricket' is very far from being a gimmick and there is a place in it for all the arts of cricket, most of which are subtle ones. **❞**

E. W. SWANTON

Daily Telegraph, 1963

❝I've never seen cricketers move as quickly, gathering the sacred stumps. The charge of the brigade over. A win for the West Indies. **❞**

BBC TELEVISION COMMENTARY

as the West Indies become the first World Cup champions, 1975

Chapter
2

· · · · · · ·

BATTERS

" Find out where the ball is.
Go there. Hit it. **"**

Attributed to **SIR RANJITSINHJI VIBHAJI JADEJA**

on the three precepts of batsmanship

" [Grace] revolutionised cricket. He turned it from an accomplishment into a science; he united in his mighty self all the good points of all the good players and made utility the criterion of style … he turned the old one-stringed instrument into a many chorded lyre. **"**

K S RANJITSINHJI

on William Gilbert (W. G.) Grace, widely considered one of cricket's greatest-ever players, scorer of 54,896 first-class runs and taker of more than 2,800 wickets across fourty-four seasons between 1865 and 1908, The Jubilee Book of Cricket, *1897*

"Admission 3d;
If Dr W. G. Grace plays, Admission 6d. **"**

NOTICE OUTSIDE GROUNDS IN 1870s

**It's Test cricket, it's tough.
If you want an easy game,
take up netball.**

STEVE WAUGH

*after seeing off West Indian fast bowlers in the Caribbean in 1995. It was the Windies'
first series defeat in fifteen years and cost them their number 1 ranking.*

" Others scored faster; hit the ball harder; more obviously murdered bowling. No one else, though, ever batted with such consummate skill. **"**

JOHN ARLOTT

on Jack Hobbs, who in 1924 became the all-time leading run-scorer in Test match cricket, a record he would hold for twelve years, Profile of a Master, *1981*

❝Perhaps it is best to say that, if all living things in India are incarnations, Gavaskar is technical orthodoxy made flesh.**❞**

SCYLD BERRY

on Sunil Gavaskar overtaking Sir Don Bradman's world record of twenty-nine Test centuries, December 1983

❝He is a fallible genius. He flirts with the record book when, we suspect, he could monopolise it. His cricket, always potent and often pure, is unwaveringly instinctive. **❞**

DAVID FOOT,
biographer of Viv Richards, 1979

"I loved the game, but I sometimes wonder what all the fuss is. It was just something I did well. A lot of people do things well. I sometimes get a bit embarrassed by the accolades that come with being a cricketer – you are just doing something you love doing.**"**

ALLAN BORDER,

who stood alone for nearly thirteen years as Test cricket's greatest run-scorer, The Australian, *2014*

"We started talking about cricket and the army, particularly similarities like camaraderie, discipline, commitment and the importance of following a plan."

STEVE WAUGH

Daily Telegraph, *2001*

"He was unstoppable. I'll be going to bed having a nightmare of Sachin just running down the wicket and belting me for six. I don't think anyone, besides Don Bradman, is in the same class.**"**

SHANE WARNE

on Sachin Tendulkar, 1998, after the little master averaged 113 against the Australian tourists

" Batsmen walk out into the middle alone. Not Tendulkar. Every time Tendulkar walks to the crease a whole nation, tatters and all, march with him to the battle arena. A pauper people, pleading for relief, remission from the lifelong anxiety of being Indian, by joining in spirit their visored saviour. **"**

Indian poet **C. P. SURENDRAN**
on Sachin Tendulkar, 1998, who leads all Test batsmen with 15,921 runs,
a record he's held since 2008. Joe Root, the current active leader,
has 7,455 as of the start of 2020.

❝I suppose I can gain some consolation from the fact that my name will be permanently in the record books. **❞**

MALCOLM NASH,

Glamorgan bowler, 1967, after Gary Sobers became the first batsman to hit six sixes in a single over

❝You begin to wonder where it was all going to end. By that stage you have tried all your tactics and your variety, it has not really got you anywhere and it begins to boil down to if he will make a mistake… I don't suppose I can call you a lucky bleeder when you've got 347.**❞**

ANGUS FRASER

sneaks one past the outside edge during Brian Lara's marathon 375 in 1994, breaking Gary Sobers' 36-year-old mark. He would later go on to top it again with a 400 a few years later, becoming the only player to score a quadruple century in Test cricket. Reported by the BBC, 2014.

" Mandela's first words to me were: 'Fraser, can you please tell me, is Donald Bradman still alive?' **"**

MALCOLM FRASER,

former PM of Australia, in 1986 after visiting Nelson Mandela
while leading an Eminent Persons Group to argue for greater sanctions
against South Africa

“When bowling to him my share of the battle was certainly not one of brute force and something ignorance. The bowler who is confronted by Bradman and doesn't think, doesn't bowl for long. Mere getting rid of the ball, leg-side bumpers for example, cut very little ice when in opposition to such a cool and practised player as Don. That fellow is a very long way from being the 'cocktail cricketer'.**”**

HAROLD LARWOOD,

England fast bowler writing in his book Body-Line?, *1933*

❝He is so dedicated to the perfection of his own batting technique that he is sometimes oblivious to the feelings and aspirations of his team-mates.**❞**

ARTHUR CONNELL,

chairman of the Yorkshire committee, on Sir Geoffrey Boycott in 1978, Stuart Rayner, The War of the White Roses: Yorkshire Cricket's Civil War, 1968–1986, *2016*

"He's my best mate.
He's been brilliant just to be there for me
all the time.**"**

An emotional **JAMES ANDERSON**
*discusses Alistair Cook moments after his last match for England,
Sky Sports, 2018*

Pope knows how to play in any situation. He has this ability to counteract any situation where he can put bowlers back under pressure. That is a real quality. He has at times outshone Ben Stokes, which speaks volumes.

VIKRAM SOLANKI,

former England batsman, on England's new batting hope Ollie Pope,
BBC Radio Five Live, 2020

It's getting embarrassing praising him every day.

DARREN GOUGH

on Ben Stokes after his 30th score of 50 or more in Tests, which includes eight hundreds, TalkSport Radio, 2020

"Diamonds like [Ollie] Pope come along very rarely. It's very rare that you come across someone who has the talent and the work ethic at a young age."

JONATHAN TROTT,

former England batsman, BBC Radio, 2020

The record still stands at the moment but I'm sure one day somebody will go past it but that was a great day for me.

GRAHAM GOOCH

on his record 333 knock at Lord's cricket ground in 1990, the highest score at the venerable old stadium and the highest score by an English batsman in Test cricket, 2014

"A great, great moment in cricketing history, as we talk the Prime Minister Baldwin Spencer, just newly elected, making his way out on the middle to congratulate Brian Lara, the England players all congratulating him. He is now 384 not out. World record score. I hear champagne corks going, what a moment. What a moment for cricket, what a moment for Brian Lara. He'll enjoy the moment, but I know he wants 400 now.**"**

IAN BOTHAM *on Brian Lara's record-breaking knock as he went on to score 400 not out, Fox Sports, 2004*

"It's really, really tiring."

BRIAN LARA

Post-match interview after breaking the world record for most runs in a single Test match innings, Fox Sports, 2004

" There goes the sweep, there it is, perhaps the most significant single ever in the history of Test match cricket. Brian Charles Lara becomes the first man in the history of the game to register a score of 400. **"**

BOB WILLIS

Fox Sports, 2004

❝ He had magic eyes. He picked the ball up incredibly quickly. **❞**

VIC MARKS,

cricketer turned commentator, on his former colleague

Viv "the master blaster" Richards, BBC, 2012

❝ He's the best that I've seen… I can't see, in my lifetime, the game of cricket talking about the people who carried the game to new heights and not have Viv Richards mentioned in the conversation. **❞**

JIMMY ADAMS,
former West Indies captain, on his cricket idol, BBC, 2012

Chapter

3

• • • • • • •

BOWLERS

❝One of the most difficult propositions for county batsman in recent years has been to try and conquer Sussex CCC pace bowler Jofra Archer. It is a proposition I have faced on three occasions with very little success. It is clear that he has an abundance of talent, but there is a selection of unique traits that make him a little special.**❞**

NED ECKERSLEY,
county pro, on Jofra Archer, The Cricketer, *2018*

"Facing a fast bowler is like standing
on the outside lane of the M1,
and when the car is 22 yards away,
trying to get out of the way.**"**

ALEC STEWART

Attributed (date unknown)

"He was, for a certainty, the only bowler who quelled Bradman; the only bowler who made Bradman lose his poise and balance, departing from his set path of easeful centuries into flurried and agitated movements.**"**

JACK FINGLETON

on Harold Larwood, Brightly Fades the Don, *1949*

❝ [Fred Trueman was] without rival, the ripest, the richest, the rip-roaringest individual performer on cricket's stage. **❞**

A. A. THOMSON

on Fred Trueman, The Cricketer, *1961*

“If you guys really want to know what fast bowling is about just wait until you guys come in to bat… You guys are history.**”**

DEVON MALCOLM,

after getting hit in the head with a bouncer by de Villiers, suggests the South Africans would regret it. They did. He took 9-57 in the next innings.

If someone's really quick and hostile, whether you've practised it a million times or not, it's not nice.

NICK COMPTON,
former England batsman, BBC, 2017

“There's no batsman on earth who goes out to meet Dennis Lillee and Jeff Thomson with a smile on his face.**”**

CLIVE LLOYD

on Lillee, 1974, Simon Hughes, Cricket's Greatest Rivalry, *2013*

❝First innings of my life, in Karachi, I thought it would be my first and last innings. In the first match, I had no idea. Waqar [Younis] bowling from one end, Wasim [Akram] going full-throttle from the other. And they had just started reverse-ball. To go there and play suddenly, I was completely out of place.**❞**

SACHIN TENDULKAR,

the all-time leading run-maker in Test history, speaking to Breakfast with Champions in 2018 of his debut as a sixteen-year-old in November 1989

" You don't need a helmet facing Waqar so much as a steel toe cap. **"**

SIMON HUGHES

on Waqar Younis' mastery of inswinging Yorkers.
Attributed (date unknown)

❝I just try to bore the batsmen out. There's no secret, really. I've always said that if you can land 99 balls out of 100 where you want to land them, just hitting the top of off-stump, then you will take wickets. It's pretty simple stuff, but the complicated thing is to keep it simple. That's what I've done reasonably well through my career.**❞**

GLEN McGRATH

in 2005 at Lord's after becoming the fourth player and first seamer to reach 500 Test wickets

❝For me that's why you play the game. There was nothing malicious about it. It was like two warriors going at each other. A bloke's bowling at 150kph, trying to rip the fingers off your hand, or even worse. It gets your blood going, the adrenaline pumping, you're in a fight – to me that's what Test cricket is all about.**❞**

JUSTIN LANGER

in 2004 on facing the fastest ever bowler, Shoaib Akhtar

" The full implications of the religious teaching may have passed me by, but there was one overriding compensation which made those three hours absolutely compulsory. We played cricket. Needless to say, I never missed Sunday School, bible in one hand and cricket ball in the other. **"**

MALCOLM MARSHALL

Marshall Arts, *1987*

"For one hour, on an untrustworthy pitch, he performed like the very devil himself.**"**

MARK NICHOLAS

on West Indies great Sir Curtly Ambrose after bowling England out for 46 in 1994

“ No bugger ever got all ten when
I was at the other end. **”**

SYDNEY BARNES

after watching Jim Laker take all ten wickets for England v Australia,
Old Trafford, 1956

❝My effort should disprove that India
cannot produce fast bowlers.
For fifteen years that has been my one
great motivation.**❞**

KAPIL DEV

on passing Richard Hadlee's record of 431 Test wickets, 2004

❝ [Jofra] Archer's spell put Smith out of the Test and is threatening to change the mood of an Ashes series in a way no England fast bowler has done since Frank Tyson. **❞**

LAWRENCE BOOTH

"England's 10 most fearsome pace bowlers of all time", Daily Mail, *2019*

"I bowled a 13-over spell that ended with the final wicket, but right at the start of that spell I didn't know what I was doing. I was all over the place and probably shouting at fielders. Broady came up to me and said, 'Get your head out of your arse, mate, stop being an absolute tool'. Or words to that effect. **"**

JAMES ANDERSON,

2013, as reported in Wisden, 2018, on his team-mates'
moral support

❝I know Dale Steyn is an outstanding bowler, but when you watch the way Jimmy goes about things, he has more skills in his locker. Steyn might be a little quicker but watch Anderson deliver those skills and it's just mind-blowing. When he gets it right, there's no more skillful bowler in the world. **❞**

DAVID SAKER,
England fast-bowling coach, Wisden, *2014*

"In an England changing room, someone is being talked about positively or negatively at every stage."

STUART BROAD

Sky Sports, 2018

❝The spell of sheer pace, brutality and menace Jofra Archer delivered in the second Ashes Test seems destined for cricket folklore.**❞**

DAVID MARK

after England's new pace bowler set a new national record for the fastest ever over, at an average speed of 92.5mph, ABC, 2019

❝[A batter has] just 0.28 seconds to decide what shot to play and to then move into the correct position. **❞**

RENE FERDINANDS,

University of Sydney's lecturer in sports biomechanics, 2019

❝I spun the ball.❞

SYDNEY BARNES,

*regarded as the greatest fast bowler of all time by the ICC rankings.
He took 89 wickets at 16.43 in 27 Tests, all against Australia and
South Africa. His 49 wickets during the 1913–14 South Africa series
is still a record, despite missing the fifth Test.*

❝The youngster down the other end is seeing his career flood right out the window. He's being no-balled out of the game. Umpire Hair is the umpire that is doing it. He's decided that his action is not legitimate.**❞**

TONY GRIEG

Channel 9, 1995. On Boxing Day 1995, Sri Lanka took on Australia at the Melbourne Cricket Ground in front of a 55,239-strong crowd. Australian umpire Darrell Hair called Sri Lankan off-spinner Muttiah Muralitharan for throwing seven times in three overs, believing the then 23-year-old was illegally bending his arm during his deliveries.

"Murali" would prove his action was legal through a series of rigorous examinations and would go on to become the greatest wicket-taker the game has ever seen, with 800 Test wickets and more than 500 one-day international wickets, making him the first player to take 1,000 wickets in the two main forms of international cricket.

"If a batsman thinks it's spinning,
then it's spinning.**"**

WILFRED RHODES

in Neville Cardus' autobiography, 1947

❝The great thing about spin bowling is that it is an art which can be learnt. In that sense it is different from fast bowling. A fast bowler either has the natural ability to hurl the ball down quickly or he hasn't. And if he can't do it, there is no way you can coach it into him. The reverse is true of spin bowling. I believe you can learn it from scratch.**❞**

RAY ILLINGWORTH

Spin Bowling, *1980*

❝ [The googly] is merely a ball with an ordinary break produced by an extraordinary method… **❞**

BERNARD BOSANQUET

The man who invented the googly and changed spin bowling forever,
Wisden Cricket Almanac Archive, *October 2019*

❝Magnificent piece of bowling from Warne. He's made a few batsman look a bit foolish over the years and there's no disgrace in Andrew Strauss looking a bit foolish but he did here. Real side spin from Warne, maximum side spin and bowling him behind his legs and not just bowling him behind his legs but bowling him middle stump behind his legs. That shows you how far that ball spun.**❞**

MICHAEL ATHERTON,
television commentary describing "that ball", August 2005

❝You need to spin the ball only three inches. **❞**

ANIL KUMBLE,

Test cricket's third highest wicket-taker of all time with 615, 2005

" The aim of English cricket is, in fact, mainly to beat Australians. **"**

JIM LAKER *in his ghost-written autobiography* Over to Me, *1960.*
His world-record 19-wicket haul against the old enemy in the 1956 Manchester
Test certainly helped achieve that particular goal.

❝What happens when you're bowling a
ball is you throw it up a bit, so in the early
stages of the trajectory there's a small
component of the airflow past the ball, where
the ball is rising and that vertical motion
against the spin will give it a small side force,
which will move it to the right a little bit…
But then once the ball hits the top of the
trajectory then that side force goes away and
then as the ball starts to come…

...back down due to gravity you now have a vertical flow past the ball coming from below and that changes the direction of the side force... So initially the batsman would be watching the ball coming towards them, and all of a sudden at the top of the trajectory it starts to come down and it's suddenly moving away from them. 🙷

PROFESSOR DEREK LEINWEBER

on the science of spin bowling, interview in The Guardian, *July 2013*

❝If you interview any spinner that played for a long time, they'll tell you [the ages between 29 and 37] were their prime years.**❞**

PAT POCOCK,

former England off-spinner who didn't get picked between the ages of 29 and 37, Cricket Monthly, *2016*

" Spin bowling is a battle of wits. **"**

DILIP DOSHI,

one of only four Test bowlers to take 100-plus wickets after making their
Test debut after the age of thirty, espncricinfo.com, 2006

"The thing with Warnie was that he does play a lot of mind games. He'd talk loudly about the fields he sets, what he thinks your weaknesses are, it's almost like setting down a challenge to your ego and trying to get you thinking about everything other than what he's really trying to do to you. Or sometimes he wants you to know exactly what he's trying to do to you.**"**

KUMAR SANGAKKARA,

one of the greatest batsmen against spin, Wisden, *2016*

" Part of the art of bowling spin is to make the batsman think something special is happening when it is not. **"**

SHANE WARNE,

leg-spinner who took 708 Test wickets, the second highest of all time,
Mike Brearley's On Cricket, *2018*

"Leg-spin is by far the hardest thing to do in cricket. The skill level is above and beyond anything else. It is just too hard to be consistent.**"**

GRAEME SWANN,
former England bowler, BBC, 2015

❝Hobbs would have been a typical county spinner if he had been born sixty years earlier. As it happened, he was for much of his career unique. **❞**

CHRISTOPHER MARTIN-JENKINS

on Robin Hobbs, the last English leg-spinner to take 1,000 first-class wickets, who retired in 1981

❝Out all night, sleep all day… and also when I was younger, quite a lot younger, was my little party piece in the dressing room, was I could get me-self in a position where I could lick me own balls. **❞**

PHIL TUFNELL

on why he's called "The Cat", Triple M Radio, 2019

"His action might not have the complexity of Muralitharan or the elegance of Shane Warne but still, in today's world he is one of the toughest bowlers to face in international cricket.**"**

BHAVESH ZUTSHI

on Sri Lankan Rangana Herath, who holds the record for best figures by a left-arm spinner with nine for 127, Essentially Sports, 2012

&&Murali is no off-spinner in the traditional sense – the close-to-the-stumps, drift and turn type off-spinner in the Laker or Titmus mould. Instead, a closer comparison would be with Lance Gibbs, the great West Indian whose wide-of-the-crease, open-chested action with huge fingers wrapped around the ball brought him more wickets than any other off-spinner until Murali took off-spinning to another dimension. **JJ**

MICHAEL ATHERTON

on Muttiah Muralitharan, the greatest wicket-taker of them all, The Telegraph, *2001*

❝ No batsman could read the ball, however often they tried to step out to drive him and loft him. He had the deception. **❞**

ERAPALLI PRASANNA,

former Indian cricket player, on West Indian Lance Gibbs, the first spinner to take more than 300 wickets and second ever after Fred Trueman to pass that landmark. He showed the world the West Indies could produce world-class slow bowlers as well as devastating seamers, espncricinfo.com (date unknown)

Chapter

4

• • • • • • •

ALL-
ROUNDERS

"This assault on the Australian bowling encapsulated everything that is most thrilling about sport: physical presence, instinctive brilliance, guts, the sense that it is all just a great joyous thrill and you might as well have a go because we'll all be dead one day...

...Of course, he came into the match having lost the captaincy after a pair at Lord's and when he came to the crease in the second innings as England followed on, the situation was hopeless.
Only nobody had told Beefy. 🙶

AUSTRALIA'S *TELEGRAPH*

in 1981 after Sir Ian Botham created history by helping England become the first ever side to win after being forced to follow on

"When you're a batter and a bowler, you enjoy yourself twice as much.**"**

GEORGE HIRST,

Yorkshire and England all-rounder, 1906

If I'd done a quarter of the things of which I'm accused, I'd be pickled in alcohol. I'd be a registered addict and would have sired half the children in the world's cricket-playing countries. **"**

IAN BOTHAM

Attributed (date unknown)

❝The first rock-n-roll cricketer.❞

LEN HUTTON

on Ian Botham, 1986

❝He lifted the game from a state of conventional excitement to one of unbelievable suspense and drama and finally into the realm of romantic fiction.**❞**

HENRY BLOFELD

on a then eighteen-year-old Ian Botham, 1974

"He had found pace, subtlety, and the psychological domination he had never before possessed. His batting became filled with a massive, easy confidence. There was no swagger: just a huge relish for the confrontation, and an inner certainty about his newly acquired greatness.**"**

SIMON BARNES

on Andrew Flintoff, "The Leading Cricketer in the World", 2006

"The greatest all-round player the world has ever seen, he was happy to stand or fall by his belief that cricket, even at Test level, should be entertaining.**"**

RAY ILLINGWORTH

on Gary Sobers, Captaincy, *1980*

❝I don't know of an all-round cricketer in my time who has been as good as he has. Many of the great all-rounders – Sobers, Botham or, more recently, Flintoff – generally bat at five, six or seven. But Kallis has batted at three and four throughout his career in all forms of the game. He stands at second slip and bowls 85mph. **❞**

MICHAEL VAUGHAN,

former England captain, on Jacques Kallis, BBC, 2013

"His Test statistics are excellent – 24.45 with the bat, 27.03 with the ball – but they do not portray the extent of his impact. And they tell almost nothing of his performance as captain from 1958 to 1963, when he resuscitated Australian cricket and cricket itself.**"**

ROB SMYTH

*on the legacy of everybody's favourite commentator,
Richie Benaud,* Wisden, *2016*

"If you could watch only one batsman, it would be him. The West Indies legend… had a presence only the great actors possess. The manner in which he changed matches was astonishing.**"**

MIKE SELVEY

on Sir Gareth Sobers, the "greatest all-rounder of all time",
The Guardian, *2016*

❝There has been no greater fascination in modern cricket than watching an over from Richard Hadlee when there was some response from the pitch or some help in the atmosphere.❞

DON MOSEY

on Sir Richard's achievements, Wisden, 1990. The numbers he produced place him top among the greatest of post-war all-rounders. Only Botham, Kapil Dev and Imran Khan join him in scoring more than 3,000 runs and 300 wickets in Test cricket.

❝Cricket is such a game of glorious uncertainty that you can never say you're going to win until you win. **❞**

SIR GARY SOBERS
City AM, *2019*

" My slogan is 'India can do it'. Thank you for living up to it. **"**

INDIRA GANDHI,

*Indian Prime Minister, congratulating Kapil Dev and his men after lifting
the country's first World Cup in 1973*

❝Ben Stokes' pursuit of miracles made us feel blissfully alive.❞

PAUL HAYWARD

reported by the Daily Telegraph, *2019, after the English all-rounder's heroic year, where it felt at times he almost single-handedly stopped the Aussies winning the Ashes series and helped England win the World Cup. His year culminated in him being only the fifth cricketer to win the BBC Sports Personality of the Year award.*

❝Incredible talent unsurpassed in the game's history, in a style never before seen; a team man who provided confidence to all around him. Adam Gilchrist had the lot, and was able to show us it all.**❞**

IAN HEALY

on his fellow Australian wicket-keeper Adam Gilchrist, Wisden, *2008*

❝Pressure, I'll tell you what pressure is. Pressure is a Messerschmitt up your arse. Playing cricket is not. **❞**

KEITH MILLER,

Australia's greatest all-rounder, being interviewed by Michael Parkinson

(date unknown)

" He's done it, he's done it and my goodness it's gone way down to Swansea. Six on the trot, thirty-six in one over. My goodness gracious, what an over. **"**

WILFRED WOOLLER

on Sir Gary Sobers' momentous thirty-six runs in one over, BBC, 1968

"If you talk to me long enough I will say something controversial. I am bound to offend someone and get myself into deep water.**"**

TONY GREIG,

1976, as reported by espncricinfo.com, 2007

" He revolutionised the game and
it had to be done. **"**

IAN BOTHAM

*on Tony Greig, the 6ft 6in South African who qualified for England via his
Scottish grandparents. Greig scored 3,599 and took 141 wickets with his off-
spin and medium pace. He was named one of Wisden's Cricketers of the Year
in 1975 but would later provoke controversy when, as England captain, he
said he intended to make the West Indies "grovel".*

Chapter
5

· · · · · · ·

MAGIC
MOMENTS

❝This has been a four-year journey, we have developed a lot. We find it hard to play on wickets like that and today was about getting over the line. Sport is tough at times. I was being cooled down by Liam Plunkett, which is not a good sign! I was up and down like a yo-yo.**❞**

EOIN MORGAN,

England captain, speaking after leading his side to their first ever Cricket World Cup win following the incredible drama at Lord's in 2019 when they won by virtue of scoring more boundaries, with the two sides inseparable even after the extra super over

"This was the most astonishing, fortuitous, preposterous climax to any cricket match I've witnessed, let alone a World Cup final.**"**

VIC MARKS,

describing England's World Cup win as the most riveting final the tournament had ever witnessed, The Guardian, *2019*

"You can pretty much divide cricket lovers into two camps: those who realise what an incredible player Ben Stokes is. And idiots. **"**

GEORGE DOBELL,
senior writer, espncricinfo.com, 2020

"Australia were not just beaten, they were annihilated.**"**

MIKE SELVEY,

2010, describes England's first ever ICC global tournament victory after they crushed the old enemy by seven wickets in the T20 World Cup

❝That this House congratulates Yorkshire County Cricket Club on its 150th anniversary following its initial first-class match against Surrey at The Oval on 4, 5 and 6 June 1863; pays tribute to its illustrious and successful history, including thirty county championship wins; applauds its legacy of high-quality sportsmanship as a leading English cricket club;...

...acknowledges the work done by the club to promote and encourage cricket across the county; commends all players past and present on their successes; and recognises the hard work and talent of everyone involved in the club. 🙶

EARLY DAY MOTION

tabled before the Houses of Parliament in 2013. Yorkshire CC is by far the most successful county in English cricket, racking up almost double the number of county championshps than its nearest rival, Surrey.

" There was a period when we had to really work hard to form a side to what it is now but now it's almost on automatic pilot. **"**

STEVE WAUGH,

Australia captain, reflects on his side's formidable run, including a record-equalling sixteen consecutive wins, 2002

❝The greatest county cricket team of all time is generally agreed to be the Surrey side of the 1950s. Their success was built on a quartet of outstanding bowlers.**❞**

STEPHEN CHALKE,
on how Jim Laker, Tony Lock, Alec Bedser and Peter Loader helped Surrey win seven county championships on the spin, The Independent, *2013*

❝The four horsemen of the apocalypse.❞

NICKNAME

given to 1980s West Indian fast bowlers Michael Holding,
Andy Roberts, Colin Croft and Joel Garner, perhaps the most potent,
and certainly most feared, pace attack the game has seen

"It was the first time I'd ever really got the whiff of danger in the nostril."

GRAHAM GOOCH,

1986, after facing the West Indies in Sabina Park

" No team, apart from [the] West Indies in the early editions of the World Cup, has dominated the tournament quite like Australia did over two editions: 2003 and 2007. "

WISDEN,

2015, on the fearsome Australia side that featured Ricky Ponting,
Michael Clarke, Adam Gilchrist and Glen McGrath among their ranks
and viewed in certain quarters as the greatest of all time

"The traditional dress of the Australian cricketer is the baggy green cap on the head and the chip on the shoulder.**"**

SIMON BARNES

(source unknown)

" A classic England Test tour of modern times. Play poorly, lose the first Test, cop a heap of criticism and then come back with an answer by performing brilliantly to win the next match. **"**

MICHAEL VAUGHAN,

former England captain, on the 2019/20 England team,
Daily Telegraph, *2020*

" We'll be watching this fellow for the next twenty years. Because he's got it. **"**

ROBERT MENZIES,

future Australian prime minister, watching Don Bradman become the youngest Test century maker. Australia would win or retain the Ashes six times in seven series during his career.

"The Great Meeting of the Whigs,
in Canal Street.
The 'National Reformers,'
The GREAT CRICKET MATCH
for $1000. **"**

NEW YORK HERALD

*Newspaper advert in 1844, for the first ever international cricket
match where Canada beat the USA, making them – for a short while
at least – the winningest team in the world*

"He's got it, England have won the World Cup by the barest of margins, by the barest of all margins. Absolute ecstasy for England; agony, agony for New Zealand. **"**

IAN SMITH

commentating as England win their first ever Cricket World Cup, 2019

137

"Wow. It's hard to sum it up. What a day, what a tournament. Everyone has done everything asked of them. We have performed under pressure. It was almost written in the stars for Ben Stokes. He's had such a tough time. I'm so proud of him and pleased for him and his family.**"**

JOE ROOT

speaking after England lifted the 2019 Cricket World Cup

" That was the best white ball game of all time. England are world cup champions. **"**

STUART BROAD

Twitter, 2019

"A sports event which utterly transfixes the imagination for an entire summer? An epic marathon which takes over a nation's psyche for nine weeks? Twenty-two days of sport, six hours a day, where barely a minute does not hypnotise? We never imagined … England 2005."

IAN CHADBAND

on that incredible summer when England won the Ashes for the first time since 1987, Daily Telegraph, *2009*

"The 2005 Ashes is commonly regarded as the greatest Test series of all time, with England fighting back to secure a 2-1 victory against Australia over a truly gripping summer.**"**

DAVID HUGHES

iNews, 2019

" Body-line bowling has assumed such proportions as to menace the best interests of the game, making protection of the body by the batsmen the main consideration. This is causing intensely bitter feeling between the players as well as injury. In our opinion it is unsportsmanlike. Unless stopped at once it is likely to upset the friendly relationships existing between Australia and England. **"**

AUSTRALIAN CRICKET BOARD

Text of cable to the MCC following the Adelaide Test, 1933

❝Test cricket is not a light-hearted business, especially that between England and Australia.❞

SIR DONALD BRADMAN

Farewell to Cricket, 1950

"England have only three major problems. They can't bat, they can't bowl and they can't field.**"**

MARTIN JOHNSON,

shortly before England won the Ashes in 1986–87, The Independent

"An innings of neurotic violence, of eccentric watchfulness, of brainless impetuosity and incontinent savagery. It was an extraordinary innings, a masterpiece, and it secured the Ashes for England.**"**

SIMON BARNES

in The Times on Kevin Pietersen's innings at The Oval in 2005

&& What a triumph it would be
if he was still batting at 6 o'clock this
evening. **🥊**

MARTIN JENKINS

*commentating on the BBC before Ian Botham faced his first delivery in the
second innings follow-on at Headingley in 1981. Beefy was still batting the next
day and led England to a 500-1 comeback, becoming the first team to win after
being made to follow-on.*

"Goochie hadn't used it much and I thought there were a few runs left in it. **"**

IAN BOTHAM

on why he used Graham Gooch's bat for his momentous innings at Headingley, 1981. Gooch scored two and a duck.

❝It's almost beyond my comprehension
how someone could take 600 Test wickets.
I know how hard I had to work
to get 187. **❞**

GEOFF LAWSON

marvels at Shane Warne, 2005

ff Ntini is rightly regarded one of the most important players in the history of South African cricket. As the first black African to represent the national team, and one of the Proteas' most successful cricketers ever, he has earned that status. **JJ**

MAKHAYA NTINI

became the first ethnically black player to represent South Africa after making his Test debut against Sri Lanka in 1998. Criticised in some quarters as a "quota selection", his 390 wickets were second only to Shaun Pollock's South African record of 421.

❝ How can you play cricket with a bloke and then not be allowed to sit in a railway carriage with him? **❞**

KEN McEWAN

after Colin Croft is thrown off a "whites-only" section of a South African train, 1983

❝Dirty money earned by the dirty dozen.❞

NEIL KINNOCK,

the then Labour Party leader, on the rebel tour to South Africa, 1982

" Carlos Brathwaite!
Carlos Brathwaite – remember the name!
History for the West Indies. **"**

IAN BISHOP

*delivers his memorable commentary as Brathwaite hits four
consecutive sixes off Ben Stokes in the final over to lead his side to
World T20 glory, April 2016*

" It took me so long to get back on my feet. I didn't want to get back up. It was like the whole world had come down on me. There weren't any good things going through my mind. It was just complete devastation. **"**

BEN STOKES

sums up how he felt at the end of the 2016 World T20 final after Carlos Brathwaite had smashed him for four sixes to snatch victory for the West Indies over England in the most spectacular and cruel way possible in front of 50,000 fans at Eden Gardens and a global television audience of millions

❝We are all in pain tonight. Ben [Stokes]
plays all three formats; it will take him a while
to come back but I have no doubts he will
have a long career and do well in an
England shirt.**❞**

EOIN MORGAN

*may have been on to something when talking to press after England's
World T20 defeat, 2016*

"This win is something we are going to cherish for a long time. We have fifteen match-winners but nobody gave us a chance.**"**

DARREN SAMMY,

West Indies captain, after lifting the World T20 trophy,
Daily Telegraph, *2016*

Chapter

6

• • • • • • • •

22
YARDS

" All you have to do is look around and watch the reaction of people walking into Lord's for the first time to see the effect it has. **"**

ANDREW FLINTOFF

on Lord's, the home of cricket and venue of more Test matches than any other ground, Ashes to Ashes, *2009*

ɧɧThere's always been, let's call it 'the Surrey Strut', which generally comes naturally to people that play here, but they still have respect for the game, respect for the opposition as well as great respect for this ground. **ɧɧ**

ALEC STEWART

on The Oval cricket ground, the birthplace of the Ashes, 2015

"Sachin Tendulkar, his first ever Test 100 was made at Old Trafford… and the five-fers, the most famous of which in 1956 [was] Jim Laker. Nine for 37 against Australia in the first innings, ten for 53 in the second, nineteen wickets in the match.**"**

MICHAEL ATHERTON

looks through the honours board at Old Trafford and discusses some of the greatest individual achievements at the ground, Lancashire Cricket TV, 2017

" A lotus land for batsmen, a place where it was always afternoon and 360 for two wickets… **"**

SIR NEVILLE CARDUS

on Nottinghamshire's Trent Bridge Test ground, 1924

"Walking off there at the end when the whole of Headingley was standing up and celebrating was a very special moment and something I had to try to take in because moments like that don't come along very often.**"**

BEN STOKES

Press Association, 2019

❝Is there a more intimidating ground than Edgbaston?**❞**

Journalist to Australia captain **TIM PAINE**
on the eve of the 2019 Ashes series. Australia would put an end to a losing streak
on the ground that dated back to 2001.

❝An Ashes Boxing Day Test at the Melbourne Cricket Ground is one of the great spectacles of cricket. **❞**

DEREK PRINGLE,

former England bowler, now journalist, 2017

❝Boycott looked round, then, as
the din assailed his ears, his mouth gaped
and he tottered as if he'd seen the
Devil himself. **❞**

FRANK KEATING

*on what many consider the greatest over of fast bowling as Michael Holding
dismantled Geoffrey Boycott, getting the England opener out for a duck at the
Kensington Oval, Another Bloody Day in Paradise, 1981*

"Perfect – if you're sitting facing Table Mountain and Devil's Peak.**"**

"Every cricketer would want to have the Kolkata crowd behind him for he certainly would not want spectators numbering nearly 100,000 baying for his blood.**"**

PARTAB RAMCHAND,
journalist, on India's Eden Gardens, The Citizen, *2017*

"I had promised myself that Test cricket will be played here again and I have lived up to that vow. It's a very emotional and exciting time for me.**"**

JAYANANDA WARNAWEERA,

former Sri Lanka Test spinner, on Galle International Stadium, which lies near the country's southern coast, 2017. It had been destroyed by the Boxing Day tsunami in 2004 that killed an estimated 300,000 people in a dozen countries.

❝Oi, leave our flies alone, Jardine – they're the only flamin' friends you've got here.**❞**

Cricket fan **STEPHEN HAROLD GASCOIGNE,**
*known as Yabba, to England captain Douglas Jardine, who was swatting away bugs
during the Bodyline Ashes series of 1932–33 at the Sydney cricket ground.
A statue of Yabba now stands in one of his favoured spots.*

❝A cricket ground where a bowler can accurately be described as running in from the Himalayas end... Worcester it isn't.**❞**

ANDY WILSON

describes the HPCA Stadium, in Dharamshala, India, where the local team is called the Dalai Lamas because the real one established his Tibetan government in exile "just up the hill", The Guardian, 2013

"It's typical of English cricket. A tree gets
in the way for 200 years and when
it falls down, instead of cheering, they
plant a new one.**"**

DAVE GILBERT

has an unsentimental view of the great lime tree at Canterbury, Kent
(he's Australian, by the way), 1999

" Cricket matches like never before.
Are you ready? 100 balls. Seven cities.
Eight teams. **"**

PROMOTIONAL MATERIAL

for a new form of cricket, "The Hundred", launching in 2020

“ I'm very biased to say it's the greatest cricket ground in the world and every player really enjoys the experience of coming here. **”**

GRAHAM GOOCH

on Lord's cricket ground, 2014

" Those who run cricket in this country, especially at the domestic level, are for the most part a self-serving, pusillanimous and self-important bunch of myopic dinosaurs unable to take anything but the shortest-term view of everything. **"**

HENRY BLOFELD

The Independent, *2003*

❝The hallmark of a great captain is the ability to win the toss, at the right time. ❞

MANCHESTER EVENING NEWS

looking back at the great Richie Benaud's commentary career, 2015

❝You have come over at a very appropriate time. Ray Illingworth has just relieved himself at the pavilion end.**❞**

BRIAN JOHNSTON

looks back at his gaffe in Leicestershire, A Delicious Slice of Johnners, *2001*

ff It is curious, how the sense of style and class will make itself felt even through a cable read thousands of miles from the spot. **JJ**

NEVILLE CARDUS

on Donald Bradman, The Guardian, *December 1928*

"The batsman's Holding, the bowler's Willey."

Folklore attributed to **BRIAN JOHNSTON**
on Test Match Special. There is no evidence of it ever happening, but that hasn't stopped it being oft-repeated ever since.

" We are mourning the death of
democracy in our beloved Zimbabwe.
We cannot in good conscience take to the
field and ignore the fact that millions of our
compatriots are starving, unemployed
and oppressed. **"**

ANDY FLOWER *and* **HENRY OLONGA**
release statement to journalists, 2003

❝You have two sides, one out in the field and one in. Each man that's in the side that's in goes out, and when he's out he comes in and the next man goes in until he's out. When they are all out, the side that's out comes in and the side that's been in goes out and tries to get those coming in, out. Sometimes you get men still in and not out.**❞**

"CRICKET: AS EXPLAINED TO A FOREIGNER"

on a tea towel in the 1970s

"I was married to cricket.**"**

DICKIE BIRD,
umpire, on why he remained single, interview in The Guardian *during
the promotional trail for his book on cricketing memories, 2014*

"There is light at the end of the tunnel for India, but it's that of an incoming train which will run them over. **"**

NAVJOT SIDHU

Attributed to Indian commentator (date unknown)

" 'He tried to do the splits over it and unfortunately the inner part of his thighs must have just removed the bail.'
'Yeah he just didn't get his leg over.'
'Anyhow he, he did very well indeed, batting 131 minutes and hit three fours, and then we had Lewis playing extremely well… Aggers, do stop it…[laughing in the background] Aggers, for goodness sake, stop it…' **"**

JONATHAN AGNEW and **BRIAN JOHNSTON**

Legendary fiasco on air in the West Indies in 1991 that left the pair in tears and unable to speak

❝I think the field is absolutely completely wrong. They've changed the field, they brought fine leg up, they put a man out for a short wide long hop. What is going on?❞

IAN BOTHAM

commentating on England v Sri Lanka 2006, just as Steve Harmison gets Jayasuriya to smash one to exactly where the fielder had been moved to

184

❝We've got a freaker! We've got a freaker down the wicket now. Not very shapely and it's masculine. And I would think it's seen the last of its cricket for the day. The police are mustered, so are the cameramen, and Greg Chappell. And now he's being embraced by a blond policeman. And this may be his last public appearance but what a splendid one.**❞**

JOHN ARLOTT

Test Match Special, *1975*

ff It wasn't something I was going to make a career out of. 'Streaker' isn't something you put on your CV. **JJ**

MICHAEL ANGELOW,

Lord's' first streaker, after turning down offers to repeat the stunt at the Grand National and Wimbledon

" Again and again we come to improve ya. . . **"**

ROOTS MANUVA,

"Again & Again", 2008 – the video of which was filmed almost entirely on the Kew Green cricket pitch in a love letter to the village game

"People think umpires have skins like rhinos, or hippos, but I think we're sensitive, we've got feelings.**"**

BILLY BOWDEN

of "crooked finger of doom" fame, Stuff, 2009

ɭɭI always believed it was one eye, one arm, one testicle, because they reckoned Nelson was one short down below as well. But I always say one eye, one arm and one lump of sugar in his tea. **ɭɭ**

DAVID SHEPHERD,

umpire, on why the score 111 was called a Nelson. Shepherd would famously hop about while a team was on that score, espncricinfo.com, 2005.

"The tough bowlers. Shane Warne, Glenn McGrath, Andre Nel. These are the top guys in cricket and I enjoy umpiring when they are around for the simple reason [that] regardless of what you do, they see fair play as the most important thing. **"**

STEVE BUCKNER
Adelaide Advertiser, *2009*

"Once, Allan Lamb brought a walkie-talkie along in his pocket. He asked me if I could keep it. I wouldn't have it because it was in the middle of a Test. But he gave it to me and it buzzed – it was Ian Botham calling me.**"**

DICKIE BIRD

espncricInfo.com, 2010

❝Shepherd insisted that games under his control were played in the correct spirit.**❞**

ANGUS FRASER,

England seam bowler, on umpire David Shepherd,
The Independent, *2009*